The eternally restless soul...

Sagarika Jauhari

BookLeaf Publishing

India | USA | UK

Presentation by *BookLeaf Publishing*

Web: www.bookleafpub.com

E-mail: info@bookleafpub.com

ISBN: 9789360940003

First edition 2024

To family, friends, acquaintances and strangers. Everyone I've ever met. For crossing my path and leaving an imprint on my heart and mind.

Mum and Dad, I hope this makes you proud.

Husband, I love you. Thank you for holding my hand always, be it through sunshine or rain.

My beautiful daughter, I hope you feel proud of your mum when you grow up and read this.

My darling fur baby Scooby, for being my emotional support forever, and for being just so adorable!

The eternally restless soul...

What it is, to have an eternally restless soul,
which aches and craves for something,
you don't even know exists.

To have a foot in this world of riches,
and another in the bottomless sea of
possibilities.

To live with a constant, persistent fear
of running out of time,
and of not living in every moment now, in the
time that you have.

To love with all your body and soul,
but to always have your eyes on the road, ready
to fly, to never be found.

To have a fire burning in your heart,
but to be ice cold at the core.

Oh what it is, a blessing or a curse,
to have an eternally restless soul?

How beautifully we smile...

Oh, how beautifully we smile, carrying a
hundred wounds beneath the skin.

A bleeding soul, a broken heart.
How steadily we walk, knowing how badly we
have fallen.

And someday,
when we stumble on our own inside,
how terribly we shatter, every particle in the
body falls apart, storms take hold of the mind.

How we've built the walls so high,
that no one can touch our buried heart.

How we push our feelings so deep,
that when they are finally set free, they consume
us like an everlasting fire.

Oh how we let ourselves die, every day, every
moment. To look strong for this world, to fit in,
to laugh, even when the heart cries a river inside.

Oh, how beautifully we smile, with a hundred
wounds inside.

The sparkles in my eyes...

Oh when I was a child,
I had the sparkles in my
eyes,
They told me to quickly
wash them off,
For they be hurdles in my
flight.

And so I washed my dreamy eyes,
Packed my bags, geared up for the fight,
And into the real world was I shot,
Where a piece of paper was the king,
Where a man was rich, if he had them a lot.

I did then swim across the mob,
And found me a fancy spot,
Years went by, and there was I, becoming richer
by the day,
Comfort my body had, happiness my heart did
not.

So I went back to the people,
Who had pushed me into the fight,
I said I wasn't happy, be it day or be it night.
And they didn't seem to care enough,
They pushed me to a side,
"You fool, it was never a delight".

They asked me to find my sparkles again,
And dream now if I may like,
but when I found them on the road,
they were no longer shining bright.

Lost and broken I return everyday,
They point their long fingers at me when I pass
them on the way,
This was never meant to be your fight, they
laugh and they say.

The rain always brings your memory...

I could never understand why,
the rain always brings your memory,

Why, the moist winds so slyly hide your
soothing smell,

Why can I see your smiling face on the hazy
horizon,

Why, when I close my eyes, and let
the raindrops kiss my face,
I feel the tickle of your
touch on my skin.

Why, when I cross my arms to hold myself,
I feel your warm embrace.

A tiny tear then leaves my eye,
And I let it flow with the tears of the sky,
but I could never understand why
The rain always brings your memories...

We are artists...

We are Artists,
poets and painters.
We cannot cage emotions
for they make us who we are.

Don't ask us to not cry,
For every tear we shed is a poem, a painting.

Don't ask us to lower our voice,
for when we sing, the trees and the birds sing
with us.

Don't ask us to give up music,
for our melodies can make the whole world
dance.

Don't ask us if we could be more grey,
For when we paint, the colours burst into a
prayer that reaches the heavens.

Don't ask us to not feel so deeply,
for it is emotions that give us wings.
Our feelings help us fly.

So don't cut them off,
Just hang on tight,
and we will fly you to the greatest of heights.
For we,
are Artists, poets and painters.

It cost me my sanity...

It cost me my sanity,
To remain sane for the world.

To be able to smile,
When the storms inside me were ready to release
oceans through my eyes.

To be able to walk everyday into those concrete
jungles,
To earn a piece of paper that rules earth and
skies.

To be able to hide the demons of fear that keep
clawing me inside.

As fear is for the weak,
It comes with a price.

To be able to lock up my book of grief
as it reveals too much, it must be burned.

It cost me my sanity,
to remain sane for the world.

Like an open book...

I let my life sit on a desk like an open book,
and some did choose to scribble,
some did tear the pages too,
where the edges stand like prickly thorns.

But there were some,
beautiful souls,
who put them red roses in my folds,
they tint my pages yellow and smell like heaven,
and I choose to let them be.

I know you fear you'll run out,
be but a hollow shell with torn memories,
but trust me honey,
If one page of your life can be branded
with the dried red petals and its tender breeze,
It will be the only page you'll ever need.

With its blues and its greens…

My soul is a gypsy,
Its nature is hovering,
It searches for the divine,
Just can't stop wandering.

I may have lived a few years,
But it has lived millions,
Life by life it was painted,
With years of experience.

The divine I've found,
I found it in the sea,
I feel like a little child,
Innocent and happy,
As I always wished to be.

This wind, this water, its depth,
Is so beautiful and serene
It reminds me that only the raw, only nature,
Is divine with its blues and its greens…

An ever-stabbing knife...

Oh yes, I have melted for you,
with you, so many times.

But do not think I've lost the spine
that holds me together.
I've been through fire,
time and again,
and risen stronger than ever.

I may not look like the mighty vast sea,
But I am the river oh so fierce,
twisting and turning,
always making my way, always free.

I could be the warmth of a blanket
on your cold winter nights
oh darling but I can too be
a stone so very cold, so harsh
in your beating heart,
an ever-stabbing knife...

The Blessing...

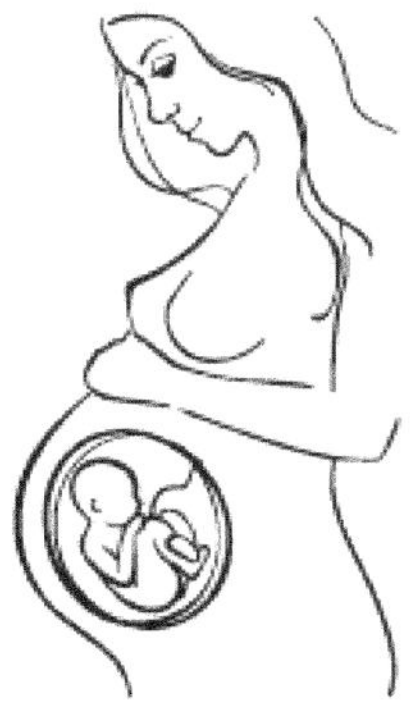

There's no greater blessing,
than to have carried you within my skin,
to have felt your tiny hands and legs, to have
heard your little beating heart, all taking shape
inside of me.

There's no greater blessing,
than to have nurtured you from my body,
seeing your tiny cheeks fill up with love,
watching you slip into the sweetest of sleep
while you lay at my breast.

There's no greater blessing,
than to feel your head rest against my shoulder,
to know I am your safe place, I am what you
know as home.

There's no greater blessing,
than to see your beautiful eyes searching for me,
instantly and always lighting up when they catch
a glimpse of me.

There's no greater blessing,
than to hear you call me mum,
for it is not a mere word that you've learnt,
It means the world to both of us.
There's no greater blessing,
than to see you grow up everyday,
into this wonderful little person, full of big
hopes and dreams.

There's no greater blessing,
in knowing no matter what happens to this
world,
no matter where I am,
I will always be your mother and you will
always be my child.

There's no greater blessing,
than the blessing that I have been endowed with,
and that blessing, my blood and my bone,
that blessing is you...

I was once in the open sea...

I was once in the open sea,
blues beneath, and blues above,
though I was an only man,
I could feel their presence, so many more.

I could see no land where the eyes could reach,
but you were breathing so very close,
an ache in my chest, a flash of lightning,
I could be yours, if you just chose.

The world has never been more full,
the mind never so empty,
The fear I feel is for my life,
the ecstasy I feel, for my soul.

In temples I have searched and in caves I have
looked,
my eyes dried out, my heart was Parched,
I only drowned in your sweet ocean,
when I burned every book.
As I was once in the open sea,
and so,
there were You ...

Oh mama, I am breaking...

Oh mama, I am breaking.
Withering away, every day...
And I know you hold my hand,
but it feels so numb, you're so away.

Oh mama, there's so many people here,
but none who can hear my cry,
And I know I need to speak softly,
but the storms of my mind don't ever die.

Oh mama, I'm so tired,
my body aches and falls,
And I know, you'd ask me to be strong,
but please don't ask me to stay within these
walls.

Oh mama, if only I could say
how I feel, open these gates,
I know, and I know there'll be help
but I fear mama, I fear it's too late.

The star-lit horizon…

The glittery, shimmering lights that
you see on the horizon,
are no longer the stars my friend,
they are the lights of the
hustle and bustle of the city.

The mighty moon no longer
lights up the sky as much,
as the streetlights light up the busy markets.

The sounds that you hear are
no longer of the chirping birds my friend,
they are the dings and clicks of lighted little
screens.

The hushed noises you hear in the middle of the
night are no longer the hustling of tree leaves my
friend,
It's the fancy cars speeding in the streets.

The faces that smile at you are
no longer souls my friend,
they are just machines,
walking, talking, earning and spending,

Mindlessly walking on the roads,
The roads which were once,
the horizon lit up with stars…

And she danced...

And she danced.
Swayed along the music like the trees dance in
the winds.

She swirled and the locks of her hair danced in
the moonlight.

It felt like madness, and it became a roaring fire,
anyone who saw her couldn't look away.

But the world didn't exist for her anymore,
A silent prayer reached the heavens,

Her moment had stopped, it became eternity.

Oh, and she danced,
Like she never danced before...

The gem was me...

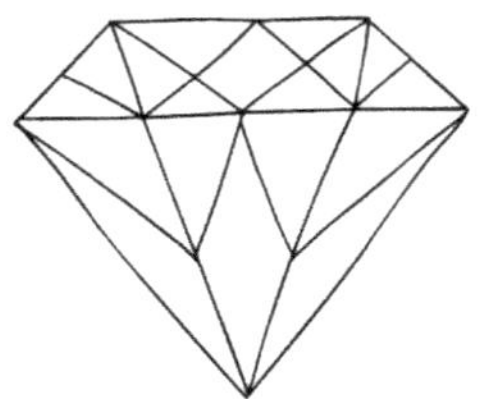

I found something so precious when I dived into
the sea,
it was a pretty gem,
as expensive as it could be.

I buried it in the sand, to get it later when I need,
and forgot all about it, when I went strolling in
the street.

When the night grew dark and no one was
around to speak,
I cried and cried looking for someone, so lonely,
so weak.

Tired and hopeless I started digging the golden
bed near the sea,
and I did find my gem again,
only to realize,
that the gem was me...

A dreaming heart was lost..

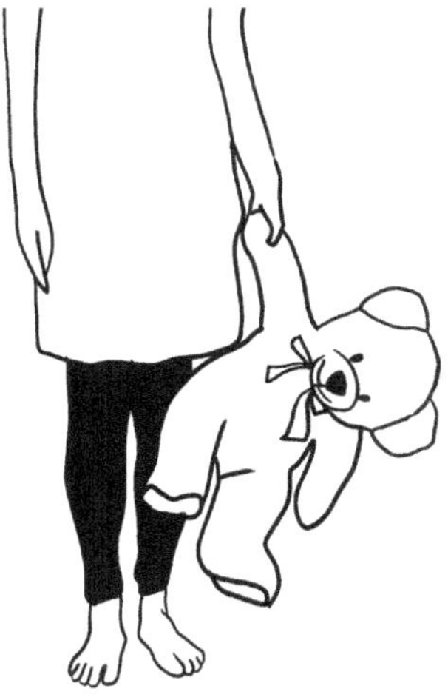

I used to believe that when the moon
Came down my window,
It brought me secrets of the dark,
I used to believe that when the cold wind
Smelled of rain and hushed my mind,
It had come to take me to places unknown and
afar.

I used to believe that in the nights,
Walked the devils and the ghosts,
I used to believe in magical lovers,
In romantic stories and perfect kisses to boast.

I used to believe I was meant for worlds
Away from this world,
For visiting enchanted lands and meeting
magical beings,
To tell the tales no one's ever told.

I may have been a mere child,
But with thoughts too loud and imagination too
wild.
Alas, the destiny was to be tamed and tamed I
was,
When a chest of stone was locked and buried in
the sea,
And a spirited, dreaming heart was forever lost.

You'll get sick of the butterflies...

You will soon grow sick of those butterflies in
your stomach darling.
And then they will fly away.

But hold on to that blanket on your shoulders
and clutch at the hands that hold it right.
As they will stay with you till the end of this
road, and when the sun's not shining bright.

Stay with the eyes that see you
in good and bad alike,
with the shoulders you will cry on when the
storms of sorrow strike,

Don't run after the butterflies darling,
they always flutter in the day,
But disappear when it's the dark hour of the
night.

A little boy once lay on sand...

A little boy once lay on sand
And saw a story unfold,
The sun and the sea were lovers,
But never was their story told.

Every morning he leaves for work,
he brings warmth and life,
While she in her magnificent depths,
Nurtures her children, a good mother and wife.

And then in the evenings, after a long day away,
When the sun starts its descent,
the winds dance in joy, the trees start to sway.

And then he meets his lover,
the golden orb melting into the blues
and with their union

the horizon celebrates,
with a mesmerizing glow
of crimson hues.

Just like that, the sun slowly dips,
And bathes into his lover's embrace.
And the world comes to the beach
To witness this moment of divine grace.

The little boy then drifted off,
to a sleep deep and sound,
The next day he must
walk to school,
Only to learn that his beloved
earth is round.

The same old "I"...

Sure, I don't live in my past anymore.
But I am guilty of visiting, more often than I
should.

Every time the tender rain touches the longing
earth,
every time the winds bring them yellow leaves
to my feet, every time I find a moment to
myself,
every time I find a moment when I lose myself.

It comes back in flashes, but I am not the
audience.
I am someone who is forced to take the stage,
to relive every minute of those days.
And it's the very same story, over and over
again.

The cheeks turning pink, the conversations so
shy,
the heart-wrenching pain, the silent screams of
why.
the same old laughter, the same old cries.
The same old you, and the same old "I".

If you were a little bird…

If you were a little bird,
You could just fly away,
If you were a withered leaf,
The winds would carry you away,
If you were a pretty snowflake,
You would fall and disappear into the ground,
If you were a drop of water, you would embrace
the ocean and never be found
If you were a tiny fish,
With the gushing stream you would flow,
But darling, you're a mighty old tree,
Rooted deep into the Earth, to the sky and sun
you grow.
So pick yourself up now, hold your head up high
Let it rain and let it thunder,
Stand tall, in the face of the storm,
You may shiver, but don't you cry,

Because darling, if you were a little bird, you
would fly away
But you're a mighty old tree,
You don't run, you are here to stay….

The demons of the night...

The demons of night take hold of my heart,
everytime I step out in the dark,
and I ask the moonless sky,
what are the secrets you hold by,
the cool breeze then whispers in my ears,
it calls out to my darkest of fears,
and I run to the shelter inside,
I bolt the doors and windows tight,
but even so I can feel them lurking,
the shadows and ghosts, silently murking,
it was then that I lit a tiny candle,
to see all vanish, no conspiracy no scandal,
and so could I hear the voice of my deep,
The devils live in you, on your mind they feed,
And so run not on the moor, stand strong right
here,
And keep a brave little candle to fight your fear.

Do you ever meet the departed again...

Do you ever meet the departed again?
Will they be beautifully the same?

Will it be the same madness again?
Will your heart beat the same?

And when they will tear you apart,
My dear will you shatter with shame?

When you walk through the fire,
will you burn, feel the same pain,
for even if you do, you know you would do
it all over and over again.

I once walked the beach barefoot...

I once walked a beach barefoot,
a night before the moon was full,
the waves were high, the ocean loud,
every grain of sand felt the Moon's strong pull...

And I felt a strange calm take over
in this night of nature's unrest,
the noise inside my mind was gone,
and gone was my soul's constant quest...

I found myself staring at the enchanting beauty
in the sky,
Majestically shining above the stormy dark sea,
and I felt a rising, an yearning too urgent,

There's a home somewhere else,
and somewhere else I do need to be...

And while I stood there, stunned,
silent like a hollow tree,
a ray of light shined, an awakening was born
Oh when this Moon so far far away,
can move the mighty sea,
it dawned,
how it moves the tiny, fragile me...

A mighty bird...he flies...

A traveler he walks all alone,
his heart of wax, his face of stone.

He is a gypsy, he renounced his home,
his blankets warm, his bed of foam.

A seeker, he can never be bound,
for craves for something that cannot be found.

A mighty bird, he flies and flies,
his quest leads him into the highest of skies.

A feeble voice he hears on the inside,
a voice so pure, a voice that never lies.

It comes from the place he left far behind,
a voice that soothes his heart, echoes in his
mind.

It whispers to him the words of wisdom,
home is his treasure, home is his kingdom.

Come back, a heart still aches for you,
with eyes full of hope, each day, born anew.

Don't turn your back now, don't you lie,
just come back home, before it dies…

So many times, I've lost who I was...

So many times, I've lost who I was,
so many times, I've wandered without cause,
so many times, I meet a stranger in the mirror,
So many times, I see my reflection and I shiver...

All those days and all those nights,
when my identity was a shock and a surprise,
my helpless self would stare at those walls,
decorated with frames from the past, where my
shadow still crawls...

I walk alone in the rain and on the streets,
I have no shoes and the reality touches my feet,

Every step I take I become someone new,
but that doesn't take away the "I" that is true,

44

And that's when I stop and stay,
I throw them mirrors and frames away,
like the raindrops that fall quietly on the bare
ground,
a ray of light then kisses my heart,
So many times, I've lost myself, and yet,
every time - I've been found...

www.ingramcontent.com/pod-product-compliance
Lightning Source LLC
Chambersburg PA
CBHW061725130726
47996CB00006B/2505